Penguins

Claire Robinson

Produced by Times, Malaysia
Designed by Celia Floyd
Cover design by Lucy Smith

01 00 99 98 97
10 9 8 7 6 5 4 3 2 1

ISBN 1-57572-137-6

Library of Congress Cataloging-in-Publication Data

Robinson, Claire, 1955-
    Penguins / Claire Robinson.
        p.   cm. -- (In the wild)
    Includes bibliographical references and index.
    Summary: Discusses the lives of penguins, particularly Emperor
penguins, describing where they live, what they eat, their mating
habits and parental behavior and more.
    ISBN 1-57572-137-6 (lib. bdg.)
    1. Penguins--Juvenile literature.   [1. Emperor penguin.
2. Penguins]   I. Title.   II. Series: Robinson, Claire, 1955-   In
the wild.
    QL696.P473R635   1997
    398. 47--dc21   97-12312
                                                          CIP
                                                          AC

Acknowledgements

The author and publishers are grateful to the following for permission to reproduce copyright
photographs: B & C Alexander/H. Reinhard, pp.7, 11, 12, 13;
Ardea London Ltd/Peter Steyn, p.4 bottom;
Bruce Coleman Ltd, p.5 top (Dr Eckart Pott), p.9 (Francisco J. Erize), p.10 (Hans Reinhard);
FLPA, p.4 top & p.20 (C. Carvalho), p.21 (M. Horning/Earthviews);
Oxford Scientific Films, p.5 bottom (Kjell Sandved); p.6 (Daniel Cox),
pp.8 & 22 (G. I. Kooyman), pp.14, 15, 16 & 18 (Doug Allan), p.17 (Colin Monteath),
p.19 (Konrad Wothe), p.23 (Kjell Sandved).

Cover photograph: Oxford Scientific Films

Special thanks to Oxford Scientific Films

Every effort has been made to contact copyright holders of any material reproduced in this
book. Any omissions will be rectified in subsequent printings if notice is given to the publisher.

Some words are shown in bold, **like this**. You can find out what they mean by looking in
the glossary.

Contents

Penguin Relatives 4

Where Penguins Live 6

Finding Food 8

Coming Ashore 10

Mating.............................12

Eggs 14

Babies.............................16

Growing Up 18

Molting 20

Emperor Penguin Facts 22

Glossary...........................24

Index 24

More Books to Read 24

Penguin Relatives

chinstrap penguins

gentoo penguins

There are 17 different kinds of penguins. They all live in the southern half of the world. Penguins cannot fly, but they are excellent swimmers. They are seabirds.

rockhopper penguins

emperor penguins

Emperor penguins are the largest kind of penguin. Let's see how they live.

Where Penguins Live

Emperor penguins live in the cold seas around **Antarctica**. This is a land covered in ice and snow.

The penguins spend most of the summer in the water. They come ashore to **breed** and **molt**.

Finding Food

The penguins are very fast and **agile** swimmers. When they want food, they dive deep in search of fish and **squid**.

There is danger in the sea. This leopard seal is a fierce hunter that eats penguins, but it can only catch them in the water!

Coming Ashore

It is fall and the penguins come ashore to breed. They swim fast under water toward the land. Then they shoot upward and land on the ice.

Penguins cannot walk fast. Sometimes
they flop onto their tummies and push
themselves along with their feet. This is
called **tobogganing**. It is fun, and quick!

Mating

The emperors are on their long journey across the ice. They travel to the place where they lay their eggs each year.

Emperor penguins have the same partner for life. Now they find their partners after five months apart. They do a dance called a **mating display**.

Eggs

After three weeks, the female lays one large egg. Then she **treks** back to sea to find food. The male guards the egg. He keeps it warm on his feet under a flap of skin.

It is freezing cold. The males all **huddle** together. They cannot feed because they are looking after the eggs, so they live off the fat in their bodies.

Babies

Two months later, the eggs hatch. The mothers return from the sea to care for the chicks. At last the hungry fathers are free to go off in search of food.

Emperor chicks are covered in **downy**, gray feathers. After a few weeks, they are too big to sit on their mother's feet.

Growing Up

Both parents travel back and forth across the ice, collecting food from the sea. This father feeds his growing chick with half-eaten fish.

The chicks grow up in large groups
watched over by adult penguins. There
are hundreds of them in the **rookery**.

Molting

As summer draws near, the young penguins **molt**. Shiny new feathers push out the old ones. Now the birds are waterproof and ready to swim.

The ice over the sea has melted.
The young penguins dive in for the first
time. Next year, if they live, they will
return here to molt.

Emperor Penguin Facts

- Emperor penguins are the largest kind of penguin. They are over three feet tall.

- Their flipper-like wings are very powerful. They can dive deeper than most seabirds.

- Emperors can live for 20 years. They have their first chicks when they are about five years old.

- Males and females look the same, but they make different sounds.

Glossary

agile   Quick and graceful.
Antarctica   Continent of mountains and ice at the southern tip of the world.
breed   Have babies.
downy   Soft and fluffy.
huddle   Keep very close together.
mating   Two animals making a baby together.
mating display   Kind of dance that males and females do, before mating.
molt   Lose old feathers and grow new ones.
rookery   Large group of penguins.
squid   Sea animal with eight trailing arms.
tobogganing   Sliding across the snow.
trek   Make a difficult journey.

Index

chicks   4, 17, 18, 19, 21, 23
eggs   12, 14, 15, 16
feathers   17, 20
feeding   8, 15, 16, 18
females   14, 16, 17, 23
finding food   8, 16, 18

keeping warm   14, 15
males   14, 15, 16, 18, 23
molting   7, 20, 21
swimming   4, 7, 8, 10, 20, 22
traveling   10, 11, 12, 14, 18

More Books To Read

Cousteau Society Staff. *Penguins.* New York: Simon & Schuster Children's, 1992.

Fontanel, Beatrice and Tracqui, Valerie. *The Penguin: Animal Close-Ups.* Watertown, Mass.: Charlesbridge, 1992.

Ling, Mary. *Penguin.* New York: Dorling Kindersley, 1993.